tutu

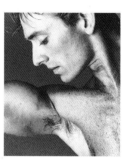

tutu

A Sue Hines Book
Allen & Unwin

I dedicate this book to my mum,
Dulcie May Barrett.
(And to my dancing teacher,
wherever he is, whoever he was.)

First published in 1999
This edition published in 2001

A Sue Hines Book
Allen & Unwin
83 Alexander Street
Crows Nest NSW 2065
Australia
Phone: (61 2) 8425 0100
Fax: (61 2) 9906 2218
Email: info@allenandunwin.com
Web: www.allenandunwin.com

National Library of Australia
Cataloguing-in-Publication entry:

Barrett, Greg, 1943 – .
    Tutu.

    New ed.
    ISBN 1 86508 542 1.

    1. Australian Ballet – Pictorial works.
    2. Ballet dancers – Australia – Pictorial works.
    I. Australian Ballet. II. Title.

792.80994

First edition designed and typeset by
Deborah Brash/Brash Design Pty Ltd
New material in this edition designed by Cheryl Collins
Changes to this edition typeset by J&M Typesetting
Photography by Greg Barrett
Photographic prints by
Brent Spencer Young/The Sydney Darkroom
Printed by South Wind Production (Singapore)

10 9 8 7 6 5 4 3 2 1

The Australian Ballet

A Monologue with the
Photographer

Why a book of dancers from The Australian Ballet? Where did it start?

Pierre Bonnard once said that the best thing about museums was the windows. Well, there seemed to me to be something of the musty smell of the museum about much of the photography I had seen of ballet. Often I found it rather reverential. It was my hope that we might open a window and let some air in, stir up the dust a bit.

Do you work with music in the background when you're making the photographs?

Preferably, no. I usually have the studio as quiet as possible, although it's a collaborative process and sometimes your collaborators may feel more comfortable with music to get them started. During the photographic sessions for this book, after the first five minutes or so no one ever mentioned music again and I usually turned it down or off.

I'd often say to dancers who wanted music that my concern was there would be no music present when people opened the pages of the book. I felt there would be more music in the pictures if there had been none in the studio.

Does photographing dance take much energy out of you?

A lot! You have to be physically fit to do it properly, to fully engage yourself in the business of it. Not because you're duplicating the moves of the dancers, I couldn't come close to doing that. But to collaborate most fully, to give the dancers the best opportunity you can, you have to invest a considerable amount of physical effort. It would seem like cheating the dancers not to. Perhaps I delude myself that my constant activity in some way assists the dancers, but I know that it doesn't work as well if I'm passive, if I'm not working up a sweat too. I couldn't do it sitting and pointing and shouting orders at people. I'm sure the results would be very unsatisfactory.

It's a bit like showjumping: if you're riding properly and the horse baulks at a fence then you continue over the fence regardless. You have to believe that your horse is going to jump. You can't work defensively with dancers and get the best results.

Do you hope people will see you in the work?

I don't think you can show yourself in the way a normal self-portrait shows you. It's not my intention to have my stamp all over things. It's more like an interpretation on the dancers' behalf.

When do you know something is 'right'?

(Laughing.) You never know! There's a feeling of something being over and done with, but I can't be much more articulate on the subject than that. I'm not looking for a conclusion, a comfortableness; rather, I'm looking for a certain amount of discord and, when the discord is right, and the visual 'balance' of the shot feels right, I suggest we stop, unless the dancers feel we can go further. Eventually, over time, the eye will come to accept the discord and the photograph will develop its own musty smell and someone will have to come in and open a fresh window.

As for knowing when the visual 'balance' is right, the best photographs should work just as well if one turns the book upside-down or on its side.

What attracted you to becoming a photographer?

I've always felt a bit uncomfortable with the title 'photographer'. And in a strange way I still don't feel as though that's what I am. I always felt that photography was so limited in its means, and the result of all one's efforts so flat, so one-dimensional and so silent. And yet these limitations are perhaps photography's strength: that your hands are so tied. Paul Klee said, 'Whatever diminishes constraint, diminishes strength. The more constraints one imposes, the more one frees oneself of the chains that shackle the spirit.'

How much do you plan shots?

I don't plan the images at all. If I plan anything, it's making sure conditions are as good as I can make them for the dancers: I don't ever keep them waiting, I don't muck about with lighting and technical matters after they've arrived, I check the studio is cool enough or warm enough, the mobile phone is turned off and I'm always raring to go when they come in the door . . . full of trepidation, but raring to go.

Sometimes I have a few images in my head and they might be a starting point. But I wouldn't bring along a set of drawings of shapes or be thinking of a piece of existing choreography that I'd seen. That would make things too rigid. It's rather that you're finding the shapes in the doing. The feel of the shoot, the excitement of the discovery and the collaboration is carried into the photographs.

So you don't feel you're compromised by collaboration?

No, not at all. Collaboration is a liberating business. Especially when you have collaborators such as I had in the making of this book, dancers of extraordinary ability and generosity. Linda Ridgway worked shoulder to shoulder with me on all that you see here. She's danced with The Australian Ballet, The Royal Ballet and now with the Sydney Dance Company. The collaboration with her was as seamless as it could be without us becoming a part of each other. I am hugely grateful for her contribution. It would not have been the same book without her. I have collaborated with Graeme Murphy many times before on photography shoots and I will always owe him an enormous debt for his generosity.

What's the fascination with dancers?

When my work was predominantly in fashion photography the models seemed to become more and more airborne in my photographs. I can remember a Vogue shoot in which I suddenly asked 14 models to jump in the air on a concrete pier out over the Sydney Harbour. Doing this wrote off 14 pairs of Italian shoes . . . I don't think the magazine ever forgave me. Making clothes look good in the air was a great discipline and that helps me now.

Perhaps you can imagine the excitement I felt working with my first real dancer, who could remember what she had done three moves back and run back through her moves for me again. That was a revelation. Dancers are used to pain and so they'll not give in until they're happy. In return for this generosity and in respect for them, I try to be as gentle with them as possible, never to waste a single leap or lunge.

During sessions for this book, some of the dancers were heading off to the Sydney Opera House for a performance that same night, so it was more important than ever to be as easy on them as we could be.

I don't think you've adequately answered the question 'why dancers?'.

The pleasure I get from working with performers may be something to do with a traumatic experience in my childhood. I was to sing in an Eisteddfod, but when I got on stage, instead of singing, I broke down and wept and had to be assisted off. Maybe I'm slowly edging back onto that stage, facing my fears.

Maybe there's a performer in here who feels better able to perform several stages removed from the actual stage. And I find the single-minded discipline of dancers very attractive.

Is having the dancers' trust important?

It's vitally important. Linda was wonderful here. She spoke the language. I was afraid that she might speak the language too well and that I might be excluded from the collaboration, but that didn't happen at all. As I said, it was a most wonderful collaboration. Some of the dancers had worked with me before and I had their trust. Or if I didn't, they certainly acted convincingly. Each shot is like a little relationship. Relationships are nothing without trust, and so it is with this process.

What sort of equipment do you use?

My equipment is very basic. Most photography assistants who work with me get a great laugh out of it. I have purposely never got into accumulating huge chunks of lighting gear, so I've not felt obligated to use all that stuff over and over again, or to use a fixed way of lighting things. I use a lot of gaffer tape to hold my lighting inventions together and from the way they look it's obvious I would make a terrible builder. For this book, I shot everything on one lens (140 mm) on my battered old Mamiya 6x7. There couldn't be a much worse camera for shooting dance photography because at the exact moment you press the shutter button, the camera's mirror flips up, blocking your view of the subject completely. So, in a way, if you saw it, you missed it.

I suspect it's another case of using the minimum, of introducing constraints. To prove something to myself I even took some of the shots in here without looking at all . . . by counting the dancer in and pressing the shutter at the moment I 'felt' would be right. The flash is firing at about a two-thousandth of a second so your timing has to be spot on to catch things at the optimal moment. I don't know where the ability to get that right comes from, particularly in someone as clumsy as myself, but it seems (touch wood) to be present most of the time.

What training do you have in dance?

None, other than photographing dancers and going to performances. I can't dance a step myself, I'm hopeless. When I was a child my mum sent me off to dance classes, perhaps to assist me in overcoming my shyness (another traumatic moment comes back to me 40 years later). The instructor was a man and he used to grab me around the waist and demonstrate the steps to me, which was terrifying. I'd hardly been that physically close to my mother! If anyone sees me dancing they should keep well clear . . . I'm dangerous to be around.

I know three dance terms, one of which I pronounce incorrectly every time. I go to the ballet often, but find the dancing more interesting if I disregard the 'story'. I suspect I am better able to photograph dance if I don't know too much about it.

Ingres said that the most important quality for an artist was naïvety. Well I hope I can continue to maintain my own naïvety in abundance. So I stick to my three dance terms. And I will never have dance lessons again.

What initially attracted you to photography?

My interest in the visual began with painters like Bonnard and Klee and Ingres, when I was much younger and more confused about what to do in my life. Theirs were the voices that best spoke for me.

It wasn't until I was 33 that I developed any real interest in photography and then I picked up a camera and could just do it. I've never read a technical book on it; but really, the technical side of photography is not difficult at all. I could teach you all you need to know technically in about an hour . . . the technical side is far too talked up, has far too much of a mystique. But I'm not sure that the other part can be taught. That's the mystery.

But you must, after two books and years of photographing dancers, have some understanding of photographic technique?

If we have brought the trick off, the technique is hidden. Technique in dancing (I hope I can speak for dancers here), as in photography, is best learned then pushed back from the conscious mind. There is no time for thinking when you are 'on': you'd be on your face in a moment if all that was guiding you was a consciously followed technique. Using technical words brings technique to the surface, so it's an advantage not to have too many of them and not to allow patterns to be established if you can avoid it. I try to come as close as I can to starting over each time, which can be a bit frightening for some clients. I always feel as though I've just started, that the best is ahead. I hope I always have that. And I hope I always have clients who trust that.

For these photographs, I pared the means down to the minimum. One lens. The same lighting all the way through. Minimal props. No trampolines. No manipulation of the images. Very few frames shot of each movement, and so on.

Do you feel that you succeeded in what you set out to achieve?

This will probably sound negative, but you always fail. It's how close we come to succeeding that matters. As a clumsy person with no dance technique, I'm trying to photograph something that I can't do myself. I'm also extremely shy (though I'm told I disguise it well) and yet I love making portraits, although it's an agony. Yeats called it the fascination with what's difficult.

For me, the most challenging dancers were those who were worried about whether they'd succeeded or not, who were still worrying when they went out the door of the studio, who were probably still worrying about it when they went on stage that night. Who are probably still worrying about it now!

Do you ever get stuck for ideas?

Sometimes. And sometimes the way to get things moving again is by changing the form you're using to express yourself.

I was stuck for a form in which to write this foreword. It seemed to be taking almost as long to write as it took to shoot the book. But I felt there were things to be said and things that I needed to try to explain about how the photographs came to be made. But it just didn't want to get itself written, it felt a bit like delivering a sermon. So I thought perhaps I should interview myself. And to make that possible, I made you up. Didn't I.

Yes, you did.

And now we can both step back into the wings and allow the dancers and the photographs to speak for themselves.

Linda Ridgway & Greg Barrett

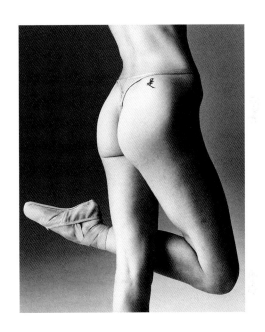

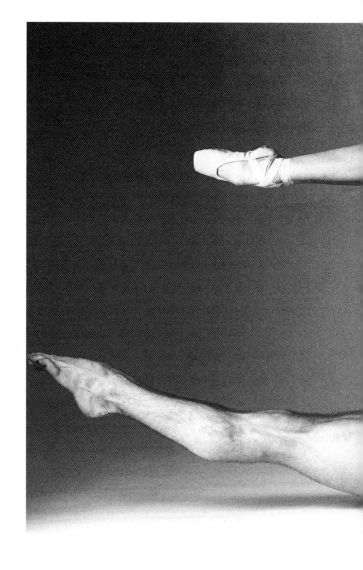

57

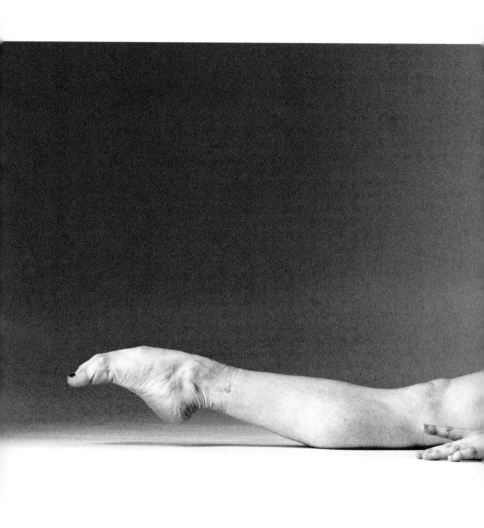

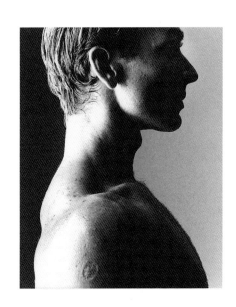

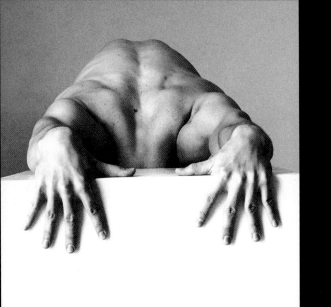

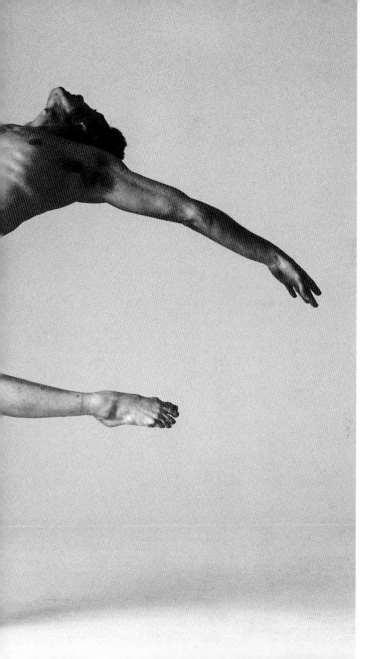

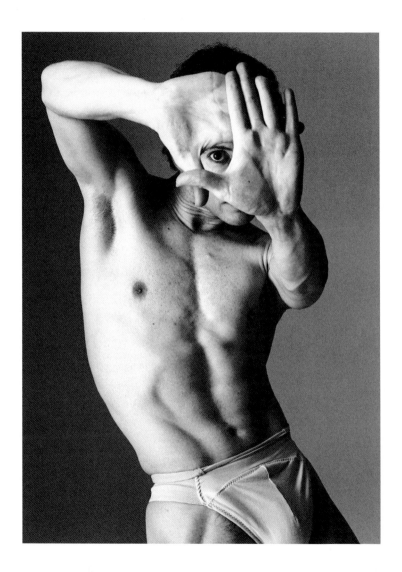

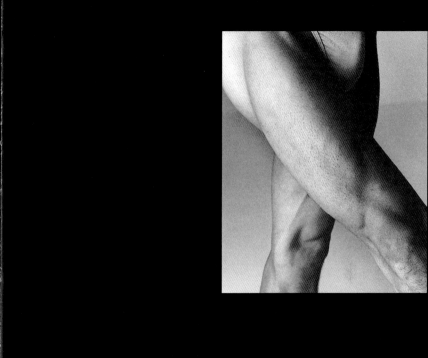

The Dancers

Page

1 Geon van der Wyst
2–3 Sarah Peace
5 Rachel Dougherty & Joshua Consandine
6 Damien Welch
7 Lisa Bolte
17 Marc Cassidy & Timothy Harbour
18 Katie Ripley
19 Shane Placentino
20 Vicki Attard
21 Matthew Lawrence
22–3 Kirsty Martin
24–5 Rachel Dougherty & Joshua Consandine
26 Shane Placentino
27 Kirsty Martin
28 Geon van der Wyst
29 Jane Finnie
30–1 Lynette Wills
32 Joshua Consandine
33 Felicia Palanca
34 Miranda Coney
35 Adrian Burnett
36 Lisa Bolte
37 David McAllister
38 Simone Goldsmith
39 Damien Welch
40–3 Joshua Consandine
44 Justine Summers & Matthew Trent
45 Justine Summers
46–7 Miranda Coney
48 Felicia Palanca
49 Adrian Burnett
50 Timothy Harbour & Marc Cassidy
51 Madeleine Eastoe
52 Robert Curran
53 Adrian Burnett
54 Rachel Dougherty
55 Simone Goldsmith

56–7 Justine Summers & Matthew Trent
58–61 Timothy Harbour
62 Claire Phipps
63 Steven Woodgate
64 Li Cunxin
65 Felicia Palanca
66–7 Rachael Read
68–9 Geon van der Wyst
71 Marc Cassidy & Timothy Harbour
72–3 Sarah Peace
74 Gaylene Cummerfield
75 Gaetano Del Monaco
76–7 Lucinda Dunn
78 Miranda Coney
79 Geon van der Wyst
80–1 Li Cunxin
82 Bronwyn Holley
83 Geon van der Wyst
84 Shane Placentino
85 Li Cunxin
86 Melanie Steel
87 Shane Placentino
88–9 Renee Wright & Damien Welch
90 Sarah Peace
91 David McAllister
92 Katie Ripley
93 Marc Cassidy
94 Steven Woodgate
95 Simone Goldsmith
96–9 Steven Heathcote & Nicole Rhodes
100 Dale Thurlow
101 Dale Thurlow
103 Rachel Dougherty & Joshua Consandine
104 Sarah Peace
105 Marc Cassidy
106–7 Bronwyn Holley
108 Vicki Attard
109 David McAllister

110 Marc Cassidy
111 Timothy Harbour
113 Geon van der Wyst
114–15 Vicki Attard
116–17 Marc Cassidy
118 Lynette Wills
119 Justine Summers
120–21 Gabrielle Davidson
122 Gaetano Del Monaco
123 Sarah Peace
124–25 Renee Wright
126 Adrian Burnett
127 Miranda Coney
128 Sarah Peace
129 Joshua Consandine
130–33 Rachel Rawline
134 Nicole Rhodes
135 Timothy Harbour
136–37 Kirsty Martin
138 Nicole Rhodes
139 Matthew Trent
140 (L–R) Sarah Peace, Lynette Wills & Katie Ripley
141 Li Cunxin
142 Steven Heathcote
143 Tiffany Moulton
144 Felicia Palanca
145 Geon van der Wyst
146 Damien Welch
147 Lisa Bolte
148 David McAllister
149 Nicole Rhodes
151 Damien Welch & Renee Wright
152 Christopher White
153 Katie Ripley
154–55 Geon van der Wyst
156 Joshua Consandine & Rachel Dougherty
158 Marc Cassidy & Timothy Harbour
160 Nicole Rhodes

Acknowledgements

Special thanks to:

Deb Brash
Sarah Burns
Anthony Clarke
Yvonne Gates
Timothy Heathcote
Sue Hines
Debra Howlett
Shirley Kirkwood
Frank Leo
Katie McLeish
Ian McRae
Josephine Ridge
Linda Ridgway
Molly Stacey
George Stroud
Ross Stretton
Maggie Tabberer
Brent Spencer Young

The team at Studio Space
Hair & makeup by Lesley Cameron

The Australian Ballet

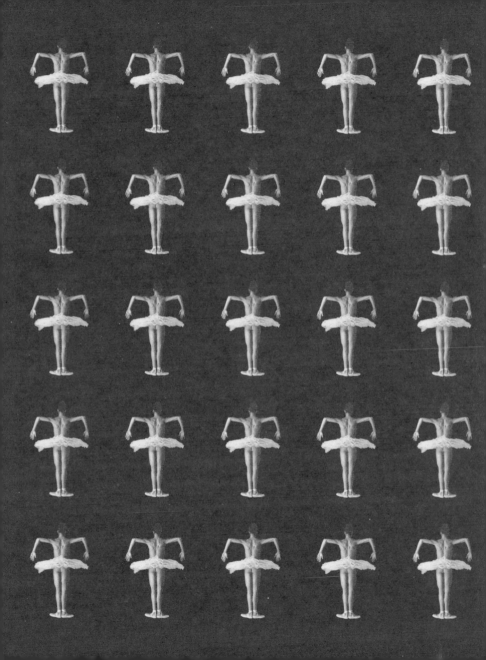